MICHAEL
JACKSON

MICHAEL JACKSON

Tim Hill

Bath · New York · Singapore · Hong Kong · Cologne · Delhi · Melbourne

First published in 2009

Parragon
Queen Street House
4 Queen Street
Bath, BA1 IHE, UK

Text © Parragon Books Ltd 2009
All images © Gettyimages

Produced by Good Publishing

Design by Gordon Mills

ISBN: 978-1-4075-4967-5
Printed in China

CONTENTS

INTRODUCTION

Michael Jackson's genius revealed itself at astonishingly early age, the angelic-looking child igniting the stage with James Brown-inspired dance routines and soulful vocal renditions that belied his years. Talented though his brothers were, and successful though The Jackson 5 became, it was clear from the outset that Michael would one day outgrow the group. He was 14 when he chalked up his first solo number one, but teen idols are all too readily supplanted. The show business annals are littered with examples of child stars who failed to shine in adulthood. Michael Jackson bucked that trend —and how.

His stunning 1979 album *Off The Wall*, complete with tuxedo-clad cover shot, announced a mature performer to the world. In reaching the age of majority he had added sophistication, without losing a scintilla of the pizzazz that had made him such an electrifying child performer. Even greater success followed three years later with *Thriller*, which not only broke all sales records and scooped seven Grammy Awards, but took the art of the pop video to a whole new level. The moonwalking, crotch-grabbing singer, with his trademark vocal tic, kept us spellbound.

Jackson may have had the Midas touch in the recording studio and on stage, but his seemingly charmed life was far from enviable. Fronting the family band when others his age were just getting to know their grade school classmates exacted a heavy price. Having lost his childhood to adult pursuits, Jackson spent his adult life seeking to recreate the magic of childhood. Repeated rounds of plastic surgery and the use of skin bleaching creams suggested a man unhappy with his identity. His appearance, affection for a chimpanzee, failed marriages, and child abuse scandals were all grist to the mill for the tabloid editors, who reveled in the eccentricities while glossing over Michael's humanitarian and philanthropic credentials.

Following his untimely death, the focus, quite justly, shifted back to Michael Jackson the dazzling entertainer, consummate showman, and pop phenomenon. His great friend Elizabeth Taylor echoed the sentiments of many in her 1995 comment: "What is a genius? What is a living legend? What is a megastar? Michael Jackson, that's all. I think he is one of the finest people to hit this planet."

CHAPTER ONE

Motown
Chartbuster

Left: A star in the making. Michael Jackson was born on August 29, 1958 in Gary, Indiana, the seventh of Joseph and Katherine Jackson's nine children. At four he joined his brothers' group, not as an indulgence but on merit. They were talented. He was special.

Above: The Jackson 5 line-up wasn't set in stone in the early years. Keyboard player Ronnie Rancifer and drummer Johnny Jackson—no relation —played with the group in the mid-1960s. Both were still there when the boys finally hit the big time, though it was as a five-piece family band that the Jacksons are best remembered. This picture shows the brothers grouped around Johnny on drums. Clockwise from bottom left: Marlon, Tito, Jackie, Jermaine, and Michael.

Opposite: Michael soon emerged as the star performer. Those who watched him were amazed by his soulful interpretations, which were, as Motown boss Berry Gordy put it, "way beyond his years." Michael's phrasing and delivery were instinctive; he needed no direct experience of the subject matter to render a performance that blew audiences away.

Below: Michael grabs the microphone and strikes a pose in this 1968 publicity shot. A broken TV set helped set the Jacksons on their way to stardom, as it was but another reason for them to make their own entertainment. Jackie, Tito, and Jermaine initially led the way, toddlers Michael and Marlon acting as cheerleaders for their older brothers.

Opposite: Michael believed he inherited his singing ability from his beloved mother Katherine, who was a gifted soprano. Both she and Michael's father, Joseph, had show business ambitions of their own, which were eventually transferred to their talented offspring. Music was seen as a one-way ticket out of Gary, Indiana, the industrial town where Joe held down a blue-collar job.

Above and opposite: Publicity pictures dating from the late 1960s. The five-strong group put in long hours of practice, both before and after school. Some of the local youths thought the Jacksons were getting above themselves and hurled abuse, not to mention the odd rock, in their direction. The family's self-belief and hard work paid off when the boys started to gain success in local amateur talent contests. Ironically, this made matters worse in the short term, since it persuaded Joe Jackson to invest money the family could ill afford in better-quality equipment.

Above and opposite: Michael, dressed in the height of fashion. The Jackson 5 appeared on the same bill as many household names, including The Temptations, Jackie Wilson, and Sam and Dave. Michael in particular would watch the more established acts to pick up pointers about stagecraft. He liked to emulate James Brown, and it was with a show-stopping rendition of The Temptations' "My Girl" that the boys chalked up one of their many amateur successes at a 1966 talent contest.

Left: The Jackson 5 (left to right: Michael, Marlon, Tito, Jermaine, Jackie) pictured with parents Joe and Katherine. Joe was a harsh taskmaster, instilling in the boys a strong work ethic and a desire to succeed. It paid off in late 1967, when The Jackson 5 cut their first records, for the small local label, Steeltown. Two singles were released, "Big Boy" and "We Don't Have To Be Over 21 (To Fall In Love)," the former in particular getting good feedback when it hit the airwaves. Meanwhile, Motown stars including Diana Ross continued to champion the Jacksons' cause, and in the summer of 1968 the group finally got to audition for Berry Gordy's renowned Detroit-based label. They were on their way—with nine-year-old Michael (opposite) the undoubted star of the ensemble—to Hitsville USA.

The high watermark of the Jacksons' amateur era came in the summer of 1967 with their triumphant turn at the legendary Apollo Theater in Harlem. This was the foremost venue for showcasing the talents of black entertainers. The brothers, now seasoned performers, won the contest, taking the eye of Gladys Knight. A year later, when the Motown hit factory was casting around for a suitable debut single for The Jackson 5, it was a song originally earmarked for Gladys Knight and the Pips that was chosen. "I Want To Be Free" was reworked and given a new title, "I Want You Back."

Opposite and above: The Jackson 5 (left to right Tito, Jackie, Jermaine, Marlon, and Michael) and Michael (above) pictured in 1971. The Motown audition represented a departure from the norm for the Jacksons. They were used to bringing the house down with their slick performances, the effervescent Michael leading the way with his fabulous vocals. Instead of tapping their feet and clapping, the Motown executives in attendance began feverishly scribbling on their notepads. Berry Gordy, who was in LA at the time, didn't need reams of analysis.

When he saw the film of the audition, he ordered that The Jackson 5 be signed immediately. Motown was not in good shape when The Jackson 5 walked through the door. In August 1968, the very month of their Detroit audition, the respected British music publication *Melody Maker* ran a piece headed, "Is Tamla Motown dead?," responding to a decline in the label's fortunes over the previous year. Vibrant new talent was sorely needed, and The Jackson 5 gave Motown a timely fillip.

Below: A TV performance in 1971. The Jackson 5 made their first network TV appearance in December 1969, a spot on the prestigious *Ed Sullivan Show*. The big time was just around the corner, yet the 11-strong Jackson family were still living in a cramped two-bedroom house in Gary.

Opposite: A star in waiting. One prescient British music journalist wrote: "Put his name in neon lights, splash him across the front page, write it in the sky, tell everybody you know… Michael will be a brighter star than anything the Milky Way can serve up."

Opposite: Michael, pictured in summer 1971. His solo career was launched later that year with the release of "Got To Be There," a Top Five hit. This was despite the group's extraordinary run of success, which saw their first four singles reach the top of the charts. Motown executives recognized from the outset that Michael's was a rare talent, and Diana Ross went a step further when she introduced the group as "Michael Jackson and The Jackson 5" on a television special. Father Joe disapproved of singling any of the boys out for special attention, but relented when it became clear that a solo career for Michael, as an adjunct to his work with The Jackson 5, would be a lucrative arrangement. It was also noted that Donny Osmond had had great success with a similar move in The Osmonds, the other hugely popular "boy band" of the era.

Above: The sweet smile of success. (Left to right) Jermaine, Michael (front), Jackie, Marlon, Tito.

Left: A string of hits and sell-out concerts meant that the Jacksons were able to swap their two-bedroom house in Gary for a palatial estate in Encino, California, bought for $250,000 in May 1971. The boys had signed to Motown for just one year, Joe not wanting to tie them down to a long deal. However, a clause in the contract stipulated that they couldn't record for another label for five years following the end of the agreement; thus the group was effectively bound to Motown for at least six years. The label also retained the rights to their name, which forced the boys to rebrand themselves "The Jacksons" when they left Motown in 1976.

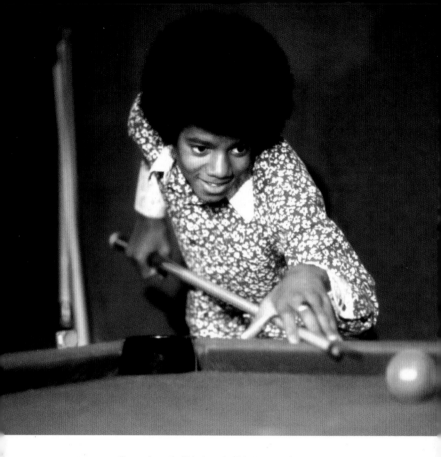

Above and opposite: Michael at work and play. He once said: "I was a veteran before I was a teenager," a fitting comment for someone who spent his formative years striving for success on the club circuit. That included some seedy strip joints, and Joe made little effort to preserve his innocence. His father demanded perfection but, according to Michael, "never told me he loved me."

Right: The Jackson 5 performing on the UK's premier music show *Top of the Pops* in December 1972. The group had made history when their first four singles—"I Want You Back," "ABC," "The Love You Save," and "I'll Be There"—all went to number one on the *Billboard* chart. "I'll Be There" remained on top for five weeks, becoming the best-selling single in Motown history. That phenomenal run came to an end with "Mama's Pearl" and "Never Can Say Goodbye," both of which reached only number two! The Jackson 5 had a string of Top 20 hits in 1972, but it was Michael's "Rockin' Robin" and "Ben" that enjoyed greater success. The latter, the title song from a movie in which a boy befriends a rat, gave Michael his first solo number one and also received an Oscar nomination. "Rockin' Robin" and "Ben" both made it into *Billboard*'s Top 100 songs of the year. The only other Motown artists to make that list was The Temptations—the label's poorest showing for a decade. It confirmed that Michael was the jewel in the crown for Berry Gordy's Detroit operation.

Above and opposite: Fourteen-year-old Michael was an accomplished, experienced performer by the time he appeared at the prestigious London Palladium (above) and as a guest on *The Sonny and Cher Comedy Hour* (opposite) in 1972. On stage he was in his element. Away from the limelight, he was struggling to come to terms with the adulation that came with being the star turn of the group. Being smuggled into buildings via the back door was already the norm, and the constraints were going to become even more restrictive. Michael would later say of the pressures that stardom brought: "I go around the world dealing with running and hiding … I can't take a walk in the park. I can't go to the store … I have to hide in the room. You feel like you're in a prison."

Above: The Jackson 5 strut their stuff in a guest spot on *The Bob Hope Special*, which aired September 26, 1973. (Left to right: Tito, Marlon, Jackie, Michael, Jermaine). The boys continued to pack out concert halls and their celebrity had even brought a cartoon series to the TV screens. It wasn't a vintage year musically, however. Joe Jackson put it down to lack of promotion, and the seeds of the group's split from Motown were sown, though for legal reasons the extrication process would take another three years.

Opposite: Michael performing in London in 1974.

Opposite: Michael, pictured with his parents Katherine and Joe Jackson, at the Golden Globe Awards, 1973.

Above: The Jackson 5 attend the Grammy Awards ceremony at the Hollywood Palladium in 1974 (left to right: Jermaine, Tito, Jackie, Marlon, and Michael). The dynamics of the group changed when Tito married schoolfriend Dee-Dee Martez in 1972, and Jermaine wed Berry Gordy's daughter Hazel the following year. The Motown boss took a laissez-faire view of such events—as long as they didn't involve Michael. Jermaine's marital tie to Gordy increased speculation that he too was being groomed for a solo career, and that seemed a distinct possibility when the group's original lead singer scored the family's best success of 1973 with "Daddy's Home," which made the Top 10.

Right: Michael, pictured in spring 1975, aged 17. This was a transitional period for the Jacksons. A year earlier, "Dancing Machine" had given the boys their biggest hit since "Never Can Say Goodbye." Disco was the next big thing and the song, which reached number two on the *Billboard* chart, put the group firmly in the vanguard. However, it would be their last major hit for Motown. Michael's solo career had stalled somewhat, too, his fourth album, *Forever Michael*, failing to break into the top 100. It was a temporary blip: 1976 would see a parting of the ways for the Jacksons and Motown, ushering in a period of renewed success.

Left: By the spring of 1975 the Jacksons' main concern was to cut their ties with Motown and start over with a label that offered greater creative freedom and the chance to increase their earning power. Michael was a lone dissenting voice, reminding the other family members that Berry Gordy had given them the platform to showcase their talent. The consensus was that the dues had been paid, and Michael fell into democratic line. The Jacksons signed to the CBS subsidiary Epic on vastly improved terms, though not all of that label's bosses thought it represented good business. Many industry insiders believed the Jacksons' best days were behind them.

Opposite: The Jackson 5 flamboyantly attired, befitting their effervescent stage routine. The move to Epic heralded a change in the line-up. It would have been politically insensitive for Jermaine, Berry Gordy's son-in-law, to jump ship and he chose to stay with Motown and develop his solo career. Into his shoes would step 14-year-old Randy, who had already featured as a percussionist and was to be drafted into the group as a fully fledged member.

Right: Michael had legions of adoring fans, yet from an early age he had a deep-seated dissatisfaction regarding his appearance. His brothers teased him about his nose and his father also made disparaging remarks about his looks.

Right: The contract with Epic gave the Jacksons plenty to smile about: an initial fee of $750,000, a minimum $350,000 per album and a royalty of 94.5 cents for each long player sold—an eight-fold increase on their existing deal. It was not all plain sailing, however. Their Motown contract still had some months to run, and the Jacksons were hit with a $5 million lawsuit for breach of contract. It was also made clear that Motown owned the rights to the group's name; they might continue to perform, but not as The Jackson 5. A countersuit was filed for unpaid expenses, royalties, and advances, the opening shots in a five-year legal battle.

Opposite: Michael, pictured in 1976. In March that year the Motown deal expired and The Jacksons officially joined Epic's roster. The new studio bosses didn't quite give Michael and his brothers carte blanche in selecting the material they recorded. But Epic gave assurances that any songs written by the group would be judged on their merits. The Jacksons' first two albums for Epic were produced by Kenny Gamble and Leon Huff, the architects of the Philadelphia Sound and the writing team behind a string of soul classics. The debut album *The Jacksons* featured "Enjoy Yourself," which made the Top 10 on the *Billboard* chart, and "Show You The Way To Go," which had a catchy melody and a great vocal from Michael.

Above: Michael, pictured with Woody Allen at a Studio 54 party in 1977.

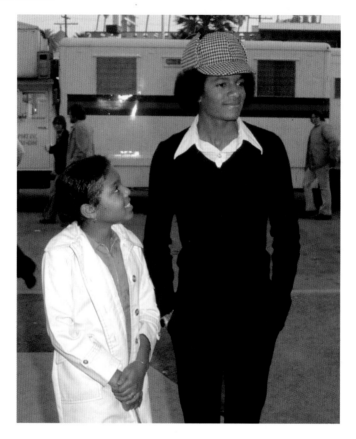

Above: Janet Jackson, the baby of the family, looking up to her famous older brother. Janet appeared on stage with her siblings at the age of seven and had a successful career as a child actor before treading her own path to pop music superstardom in the mid-1980s.

Opposite: Michael, pictured onstage during a Jacksons TV special, November 1978. The group was at a crossroads. The first two albums for Epic hadn't sold well, and Michael's solo career was on hold. The Jacksons had already played Las Vegas, and although the show was a tour de force, it raised thoughts that they might become a cabaret act rehashing their old hits. Epic's parent company CBS was considering pulling the plug, but agreed to let them work on a third album with much greater artistic control.

CHAPTER TWO

Destiny
Fulfilled

Above: Diana Ross had taken Michael under her wing almost as soon as The Jackson 5 signed to Motown. In 1977 the close friends performed together in *The Wiz*, an all-black reworking of the Wizard of Oz story. Michael revelled in taking on the role of Scarecrow, to Diana's Dorothy, but the lasting legacy of the film was the impact it had on his solo career. The movie's musical director was Quincy Jones, who had worked with many big band legends in his 30-year career, and was an acclaimed film composer. Michael was itching to break out of the confines of the group and reignite his solo career, and in 1979 he took up Jones's offer of help. It proved to be a match made in heaven.

Opposite: Michael, pictured at a rock & roll sports event in Los Angeles, 1978. The Jacksons released *Destiny* that year, a terrific self-produced and mostly self-written set widely regarded as the group's best album. It yielded two show-stopping singles, "Blame It On The Boogie" and "Shake Your Body (Down To The Ground)," which reverberated round the disco halls worldwide, but *Destiny*'s success didn't deter Michael from wanting to develop as a solo artist.

Above: Attending the New York premiere of *The Wiz*. The film was not a great commercial success but it gave Michael a valuable insight into the movie-making process, which would stand him in good stead when he turned his hand to making pop videos for the MTV age.

Opposite: A studio portrait, July 1978. The entertainment business dominated Michael's life, both as a consumer—watching movies featuring the likes of Sammy Davis Jr., Fred Astaire, and Gene Kelly—and, of course, as a producer. "My goal in life is to give the world what I was lucky to receive … the ecstasy of divine union through my music and my dance."

Opposite and right: Michael putting his heart and soul into a number during the Destiny tour. Raw emotion got the better of him on numerous occasions during the making of *Off The Wall*. Michael struggled to get through a take of "She's Out Of My Life" without breaking into tears. Finally, Quincy Jones decided to leave the quivering vocal on the recording of this heart-rending ballad, which became the fourth hit single to be culled from the album.

Above: Sharing a backstage joke with Jackie during the grueling Destiny tour, which began in January 1979 and ran through to September the following year. The Jacksons took in Europe and Africa, though the main leg of the tour involved traversing the States, taking in 80 cities. Michael's *Off The Wall* album, which would eventually sell 10 million copies, was released during the tour, and the set list was amended to incorporate some of its smash hits, including the title track.

Opposite: Michael photographed during the Destiny tour.

Above and opposite: On stage with his brothers during the Destiny tour, 1979. The fans may have loved the show and the new songs, but Michael wasn't quite so enamored. He felt that they hadn't progressed enough, that the new album didn't represent any great departure from their output during the Motown era. The answer lay in a new solo venture. The CBS bosses had granted the Jacksons greater autonomy in the making of *Destiny*; now he would seek the same license to express himself and expand as an artist.

Left and opposite: Putting on the style at the Municipal Auditorium, New Orleans, during the Destiny tour. It was a defining year for Michael, one which took his career to a new level. The *Off the Wall* album topped the album charts and yielded four Top 10 hit singles, including "Don't Stop 'Til You Get Enough" and "Rock With You," both of which reached number one on the *Billboard* Hot 100. Producer Quincy Jones marveled not only at how accomplished Michael was as a vocalist, but at his professionalism and dedication. When the album was in the can he had little doubt that here was the star of the next decade and beyond.

Left and opposite: These 1979 portraits reflect the two faces of Michael Jackson: shy, diffident and self-aware when not performing; exuding boundless confidence and brio when in stage mode. *Off The Wall* was released in August that year, when the Jacksons were preoccupied with the Destiny tour. The set was a finely crafted tapestry of soul, funk, and lush ballads; an amalgam of hooky melodies and driving rhythms. Michael Jackson had just turned 21, and this album announced to the world that he had come of age. Even the sleeve image—tuxedo-clad with black tie—was deliberately chosen to mirror the sophistication and maturity of the content.

Above: Michael with Tatum O'Neal in 1979. Michael described Tatum O'Neal as his first real girlfriend. Tatum was five years younger, just 13 when the two met in 1975, and already an Oscar-winning actress. Apart from gaining celebrity status at a tender age, the two also had in common a difficult relationship with a parent, in Tatum's case with her mother, actress Joanna Moore. Their recollections of the nature of the teenage relationship didn't tally, however. Michael described it as a romance, Tatum as a platonic friendship.

Opposite: In concert at London's Rainbow Theatre, February 1979. Family loyalty led Michael to continue performing with his brothers, though they became aware that he was distancing himself from the group. It was thought—wrongly—that he would return to the fold contented after his solo project was completed.

Left: Michael, pictured in 1980, the start of the decade that would elevate him from pop sensation to music icon. There was an inauspicious start to the era as *Off The Wall* was all but overlooked at the Grammies. Michael did pick up the Best Male R&B Vocal Performance for "Don't Stop 'Til You Get Enough," which he regarded as a disappointing return, given that the album was flying off the shelves. He felt slighted that such a runaway success hadn't got the recognition it merited from his peers.

Opposite: With Brooke Shields at the Academy Awards, 1981. Shields was in the spotlight at a younger age even than Michael, gravitating from modeling to acting. Her career stalled in the early 1980s, but the two remained firm friends, casually dating but without romantic intent.

Left: Heading into the studio for a collaborative date with Paul McCartney. Michael had included a McCartney song, "Girlfriend," on *Off The Wall* and it was no surprise when the two musical giants teamed up again during the making of *Thriller*. The result was "The Girl Is Mine," written by Jackson but very much in the mold of a classic McCartney ballad. It was the first single to be released from the album, reaching number two in America. Some time later, Michael asked Paul how best to invest the money that was rolling in. McCartney, still nursing burnt fingers over the ownership of his own material, recommended music publishing. Jackson subsequently splashed out $53 million to purchase ATV Music, which owned the Lennon-McCartney catalogue.

Opposite: Michael Jackson with the "queen of disco," Donna Summer.

Opposite: Michael working on the video to accompany "Beat It." The memorable videos that accompanied *Thriller* were produced in the months following the album's release. First came *Billie Jean*, which had the sidewalk light up as it received Michael's footfall. It confirmed what we already knew: that there was magic in those twinkling feet. Then came *Beat It*, which had Michael playing peacemaker to two warring gangs, a nod toward *West Side Story*. Real gang members were recruited as extras to add to the brooding atmosphere of urban menace. But the *piece de resistance* was the mini-feature made to promote the title track. John Landis was brought in to direct this homage to the horror movie genre, which saw Jackson transform into a werewolf and dance with the undead. A voice-over from master of the macabre Vincent Price rounded out a video classic, though it didn't go down too well with church leaders, who disapproved of its perceived dabbling in occult practices. The kids loved it, though, and a disclaimer was added to appease any who might be offended.

Right: Michael pictured wearing the red jacket used in the video accompanying "Beat It."

77

Above and opposite: Michael with Cher on the night *Dreamgirls* opened in Los Angeles, March 1983. The musical was based on the story of Motown, which celebrated its 25th anniversary that year. Michael performed at the show that marked the event, a television spectacular that was recorded in March and aired two months later (opposite). It was in his breathtaking rendition of "Billie Jean" that he first showed off the moonwalk, which became his signature dance move. Recalling that show-stopping performance at the singer's memorial service, Berry Gordy commented: "Michael Jackson went into orbit and never came down."

Opposite and above: Michael and Liberace. Liberace, himself a consummate showman, would no doubt have appreciated Michael's stagecraft and the magnetic hold he had over his audience. Away from the spotlight, however, there was some upheaval. Michael severed the legal ties that bound him to the Jacksons; he could continue to record with his brothers, but was under no obligation to do so. And his long-standing dissatisfaction regarding his appearance came to a head at the beginning of the decade when he finally opted to go under the surgeon's knife for rhinoplasty.

Above: Michael's reaction to what he saw as an industry snub to *Off The Wall* was typically combative: he would put together an even better album, one that was impossible to overlook. Much the same team was reconvened, with Quincy Jones again producing. One of the key members was Rod Temperton, who had enormous success as a writer-performer with Heatwave before being recruited by Michael to work on *Off The Wall*. Temperton provided three songs for that masterwork, including "Rock With You" and the title track. He would make a similar contribution to the new album, *Thriller*, whose sales would dwarf even those of its predecessor.

Opposite: Michael carrying child actor Emmanuel Lewis and flanked by his brothers. Don King (far right), most famous for his flamboyant match-making in the world of pugilism, was drafted in to promote the Jacksons' much vaunted reunion tour in 1984. Michael had not performed with his brothers since the Triumph tour of 1981. His solo spots were the most eagerly awaited parts of the show back then, and even more so in the post-*Thriller* era.

Opposite: Liza Minnelli, pictured with Michael during her sold-out tour of 1983, was a regular consort on the party circuit. Her mother, Judy Garland, came from the Tinsel Town era of which Michael was a huge fan.

Above: Dream team—Michael Jackson and Quincy Jones basking in glory, having put together an album that topped the US charts for 37 weeks, produced four number one singles and would eventually chalk up sales of 50 million. Eight Grammies at the 1984 awards ceremony provided guest presenter Mickey Rooney with all the ammunition he needed for a neat one-liner: "It's a pleasure doing the Michael Jackson Show."

Left: In February 1983 Michael was presented with a platinum disk for *Thriller*. The album yielded seven Top 10 hits in 1983, chart dominance the like of which hadn't been seen since the days of Beatlemania. It wasn't just CBS executives who rubbed their hands at the sales avalanche. The music business was in the doldrums, and even the other labels welcomed the success of *Thriller*, which played a significant part in pulling the industry out of a trough.

Opposite: Michael, pictured with acclaimed actress Jane Fonda, who was a fan as well as a close friend. She said of his work: "The music is energetic and it's sensual. You can dance to it, work out to it, make love to it, sing to it. It's hard to sit still to." Fonda had a notoriously difficult relationship with her father, Henry, mirroring Michael's antipathy for Joe, which continued into adulthood.

Opposite: Brooke Shields and Diana Ross (following pages) share Michael's triumph at the 1984 American Music Awards, where he picked up eight awards. Michael finally got to work with Diana Ross in 1982, writing and producing the hit single "Muscles" that featured on her *Silk Electric* album. The song title came from Michael's pet snake, though the accompanying video gave a more literal interpretation of the lyric, with plenty of beefcake on show. Though he was at the height of his powers, Jackson remained in awe of the Motown legend, somewhat reticent when it came to directing her in the studio.

Above: Michael poses with actor Yul Brynner in February 1984.

Left: Brooke Shields joins Michael as he lines up with his brothers once again, an event which created huge excitement in media circles. The stratospheric success of *Thriller* signaled the end of Michael's involvement in the group—almost. There was one glorious finale, the 1984 *Victory* album and tour. Jermaine returned to the fold, the only time that all six Jacksons appeared on record and on stage together. Tickets for the 55-date tour were like gold dust, despite the steep $30 cover price and a block-booking system which required them to be sold in batches of four. Eleven-year-old Ladonna Jones spoke for many when she wrote to a newspaper, saying that she was desperate to see the show but an outlay of $120 left her without hope. Michael, who had been against the ticketing arrangements from the outset, was moved to issue a statement on the eve of the tour stating that he had asked for the system to be changed, and that his earnings from the tour, around $5 million, would be donated to charity. There was a happy ending for Ladonna, who was a VIP guest when the show rolled into Dallas.

Above and opposite: Stepping out with Brooke Shields, New York, 1984. It was a case of another day, another honor as Michael attended a ceremony at the American Museum of Natural History to mark his entry into the *Guinness Book of Records*. In just over a year *Thriller* had become the best-selling album of all time; it would clock up another million sales in the week following the Grammy Awards, which took place three weeks later. With a royalty rate of $2 per unit, among the best in the business, it meant there was serious money to accompany the critical acclaim.

Above and opposite: The 1984 Grammy Awards reflected the tour de force that was *Thriller*. The fact that hundreds of songs were whittled down to just nine was an inbuilt quality control mechanism. Michael contributed three songs, as well as "The Girl Is Mine," "Beat It," and "Billie Jean" —both number one singles—and "Wanna Be Startin' Somethin'," which railed against malicious gossip and falsehood. The rumor mill had already raised the subject of his sexuality, and over the following years Michael would find himself the subject of much hurtful speculative comment.

Right: Michael Jackson and Quincy Jones had their differences during the making of *Thriller*. One bone of contention surrounded "Billie Jean," which the producer thought too insubstantial for the set. Michael won that argument, and also insisted on keeping the title, rejecting concerns that people might think tennis legend Billie Jean King might be the subject, and Jones's suggestion that it be titled "Not My Lover." Jackson was vindicated when "Billie Jean" not only went to number one in the Hot 100 but took fourth spot in the top-selling singles of the year. That was the highest showing of the seven 45s culled from the album, though not quite Michael's best return: "Say Say Say," his duet with Paul McCartney, was second in *Billboard*'s top hundred songs of 1983.

Left: Out on the town with Liza Minnelli, New York. Michael was the hottest ticket in town, but one corner of the globe was steadfastly trying to stem the tide of Jacksonmania. Russia had a long history of condemning what one newspaper called "empty and senseless Western music." Much negative propaganda was issued by the government, but the kids were not influenced by that. When the resident vocalist in one nightclub belted out some of the hits from *Thriller* to wild applause, it became clear that the Politburo was fighting a losing battle.

Left and opposite: Michael on stage at Madison Square Garden in August 1984. Two million people packed the concert halls to see Michael back on stage with his brothers in the Victory tour, which began in Kansas in July and ended in December in Los Angeles.

Right and following pages: The Jacksons perform at Madison Square Garden. Somewhat surprisingly, no songs off the new album were included in the set, apparently at Michael's behest. Thus there was no "State Of Shock," the album's big single release featuring guest vocalist Mick Jagger. That reached number three on the *Billboard* chart, while the follow-up "Torture" also broke the Top 20. As the album racked up platinum sales, the tour progressed somewhat uneasily. Michael had been reticent about the project from the start, even suggesting it should be renamed The Final Curtain. He was outvoted, but it showed that he regarded this as the end of the line, not the beginning of a new chapter.

Opposite and below: Michael performing at the Texas Stadium, Dallas (opposite), and with the Jacksons at the Arrowhead Stadium, Kansas (below). Though Michael was a peerless performer on stage, he was also a perfectionist, always wanting to do another take to see if he could top his previous effort. In that regard, pop videos appealed to him more than live shows. Remarkably, he even cast a self-critical eye on his performance at the Motown silver anniversary special, which won universal acclaim for its virtuosity. During the Victory tour the Jacksons were offered a multi-million-dollar deal to tape the show for the home video market. Michael's was the lone dissenting voice.

Left: With eight songs from *Off The Wall* and *Thriller*, not to mention all the Jacksons' songs in which Michael took the lead vocal, it was clear that the latest gathering of the clan was hardly a meeting of equals. The show's content was a reflection of who the fans had come to see. It was a fabulous spectacle, the razzmatazz and techno-wizardry complementing the amazing aural feast. Discerning reviewers noted that the brothers were effectively reduced to bit-part players in their own show, but the delirious fans were oblivious to the fraternal tensions that grew during the five-month-long tour.

Opposite: On stage in East Rutherford, New Jersey, USA, in July 1984.

Below: President Ronald Reagan and the First Lady receive Michael at the White House in May 1984 to honor him for his charity work. Three months earlier, the President had sent Michael a personal message following an accident that befell him during the making of a Pepsi-Cola commercial. Pyrotechnics were part of the script, which had Michael singing a reworked version of "Billie Jean." Setting Michael's hair alight wasn't. He suffered second degree burns, and it is believed an addiction to painkillers can be traced back to this period. Facing litigation, Pepsi-Cola offered $1.5 million by way of reparation, which Michael donated to the burns unit at Brotman Memorial Hospital, which was named in his honor.

Opposite: Immortalized in wax. Michael poses next to his resplendent effigy at Madame Tussauds in 1985. The famous museum would produce many more "incarnations" of the singer over the years to match his current look. When the This Is It tour was announced in early 2009, the sculptors got to work yet again, using the concert posters to produce a thirteenth waxwork model.

Right: Arriving at the 1986 American Music Awards with Elizabeth Taylor. Michael seemed to gravitate towards those who understood the pressures of being in the public eye from a young age. Elizabeth Taylor became a star at the age of 12 when she took the lead role in *National Velvet*, and said that she, too, had a difficult relationship with her father, which gave their friendship further common ground. When distasteful rumors about Jackson began to circulate, Taylor leapt to his defense: "He is the least weird man I have ever known. He is highly intelligent, shrewd, intuitive, understanding, sympathetic, generous."

Opposite and above: Michael enjoying himself at the 1986 Grammy Awards, posing with fellow USA For Africa stars Dionne Warwick, Stevie Wonder, and Lionel Richie. It was Harry Belafonte who had had the idea for black artists to stage a concert for famine relief in Africa. That evolved into a song, an American equivalent to the charity single "Do They Know It's Christmas?," which had enjoyed phenomenal success in the UK. Jackson and Richie teamed up to write "We Are The World," and with Quincy Jones producing, the result was an anthem whose impact was comparable to the Beatles' "All You Need Is Love" two decades earlier. The song was recorded at A & M's Hollywood studios on January 28, 1985, and became the second-best seller of the year on the *Billboard* chart, just losing out to Richie's "Say You, Say Me." Combined sales of the single and accompanying album would raise over $40 million by the time the 1986 Grammies were held. Jackson and Richie took their bow at that event, winning in the Song of the Year category.

Opposite and right: At the time of the 1986 Grammy Awards Michael was not merely a superstar of the entertainment field but one of the most famous people on the planet. Such celebrity inevitably brought a thirst for Jackson-related stories in the media. Michael jealously guarded his privacy, and his reluctance to play the media game gave rise to an industry of rumor and speculation. One of the first bombshells landed seven months later, in September 1986, when the *National Enquirer* printed a picture showing Michael lying in an oxygen chamber. The accompanying article suggested that the star planned to live to 150 years old by sleeping in the contraption. It seems that Michael dreamed up the story as a PR stunt, a harmless piece of self-publicity that backfired badly.

CHAPTER THREE

Black or White

Opposite: Michael, pictured with Sean Lennon, November 1986. By now Michael was the proud owner of the Lennon-McCartney catalogue. Paul didn't take kindly to the news of the purchase, and relations between the two soured. McCartney was further put out when Michael allowed "Revolution" to be used in a Nike advertisement. "All You Need Is Love" and "Good Day Sunshine" also became promotional jingles. McCartney felt it was demeaning to use his and John's music in such a way, no matter how lucrative such deals were. Michael maintained that he was legitimately trying to recoup his investment, and pointed out that using the songs in such a way would introduce Beatles music to a new generation.

Above: Filming the 1987 *Bad* video, which was directed by Martin Scorsese. Topping *Thriller* was a near impossibility, but Michael showed that the five-year gap between the two albums had been time put to good use. Explaining the lengthy hiatus, Jackson said: "Quincy and I decided that this album should be as close to perfect as humanly possible. A perfectionist has to take his time. He can't let it go before he's satisfied. He can't. When it's as perfect as you can make it, you put it out there. That's the difference between a number 30 record and a number one record that stays number one for weeks." *Bad* went straight to the top, holding that spot for six weeks in America. It producing several chart-topping singles, including "I Just Can't Stop Loving You," "The Way You Make Me Feel," "The Man In The Mirror," and "Dirty Diana," as well as the title track.

Above: Filming the *Bad* video. The video revisited the theme of teen angst and urban rebelliousness, albeit with a different perspective from *Beat It*. Michael plays a privately educated kid trying to convince his friends that he can still cut it on the streets. Naturally, the subway scenes, filmed in Brooklyn, feature some slick moves from Michael and his leather-clad acolytes. He does enough to assure the doubters that he is still "bad," and the feature ends with a brotherly handshake. The video was based on a real-life incident involving a prep-school student from Harlem who was gunned down by a policeman. It was also noteworthy in that the cast included Geron Candidate, the street dancer known as "Casper," from whom Michael learnt the moonwalk.

Opposite: Michael in the "preppy" outfit he wore for the *Bad* video. For the scenes in which he attempts to convince his nemesis, played by an emerging Wesley Snipes, that he is as street-smart as ever, Michael is decked out in leather, with a mean, moody expression to match. When Snipes's character leaves at the end, content with what he has seen, Michael reverts to his scholarly style. Many critics found the video unconvincing, but it was another MTV winner and Jackson had his eighth *Billboard* number one on his hands.

The Bad tour kicks off in Japan in September 1987. Jackson ... m in Japan that he was dubbed "Typhoon Michael. "The tour ... he end of January 1989, a 16-month extravaganza that took in ... well America, where Michael did over 50 shows. July 1988 saw ... olo artist in Britain for the first time. All the UK concerts were ... ped. Even the biggest venues—including Wembley Stadium and ... uld not house all the fans desperate to see their idol perform. ...00 packed out Aintree, home of the famous Grand National ... e highest attendance figure of the entire tour, though Michael ... the fact that he was in the Beatles' home city, a place that held a ... tural map.

Opposite: With Sophia Loren and Sylvester Stallone at the American Cinema Awards, 1987. Michael may have carefully guarded his privacy but awards events, and the recognition they bestowed, meant a lot to him. Even after almost two decades of unbroken success, Michael felt insecure about his place in the pop pantheon. It played on his mind as to whether he was bigger than Madonna, or even Elvis. The doubts surfaced again when *Bad* was overlooked at the 1988 Grammy Awards, a crushing blow to his ego.

Above: Michael pictured in 1987. Michael was earning big money but he was spending big, too. A cleft chin was the result of yet another visit to the cosmetic surgeon; there were the vast charity donations, which ran to millions of dollars. Soon after this picture was taken, Michael secured the purchase of a sprawling 2,700-acre estate in Santa Barbara. This would become his private adventure playground, complete with zoo, Ferris wheel, and all manner of attractions. One of the first tasks was to rename the property: Neverland.

Above: Michael is among the honored guests as the glitterati turn out at the United Negro College Fund award ceremony of 1988. Michael was full of praise for the philanthropic organization that had been supporting black students through their college careers for over 40 years. He was also a generous benefactor. In 1986 he gave UNCF $1.5 million to establish a scholarship endowment, and donated a further $600,000 during the Bad tour, the entire proceeds of one of the Madison Square Garden concerts. In 1988 he was given the Frederick D Patterson award, UNCF's highest honor, named after its founding father. To this day, dozens of students each year benefit from scholarships funded by Michael Jackson's extraordinary munificence. Pictured (left to right) Elizabeth Taylor, Liza Minnelli, Michael Jackson, Whitney Houston and guest.

Opposite: Michael and Whitney Houston.

Above: Whitney Houston congratulates Michael on his becoming an honorary Doctor of Humane Letters, a degree conferred on him by UNCF in March 1988.

Opposite: Michael's own education was inevitably affected as The Jackson 5 focused their efforts on breaking into the big time, but UNCF's motto undoubtedly resonated with him: "A mind is a terrible thing to waste."

Opposite and right: Michael pictured during the second leg of the Bad tour, which was a stunning success, breaking box office records by grossing $125 million. Fans were treated to a visual as well as vocal feast. There was a dazzling laser show, smoke clouds, and choreographed explosions; and there was also the sight of the star flying by wire, with obvious parallels to his fictional hero Peter Pan.

Opposite: Well over four million people clapped, cheered, and screamed their appreciation and adulation of Michael Jackson during the Bad tour (shown here in Minnesota). For one so loved and admired, Michael did not regard himself as being blessed in his personal life. In *Moonwalk*, the autobiography published while the tour was in full flow, Jackson gave a caveat to the general perception of fame and wealth. "People think you're lucky, that you have everything. They think you can go anywhere and do anything, but that's not the point. One hungers for the basic stuff." He also described himself as "one of the loneliest people in the world."

Above: Michael on stage in New York with Tatiana Thumbtzen during the Bad tour.

Above: Michael and Princess Diana in July 1988. The fifth number one from *Bad* was "Dirty Diana," a Jackson-penned song about a girl who was "every musician's fan after the curtain comes down." Ever mindful of the feelings of others, Michael anguished over including a song about groupies in the set for the Wembley concert when he knew that Diana, Princess of Wales would be in the audience. He needn't have worried; Princess Diana said she loved the song and wanted him to do it. Such sensitivity tended not to make the pages of the tabloids, nor did the vast sums Michael donated to charity as the show circumnavigated the globe. The media reveled in stories that fitted the "Wacko Jacko" template; his acts of graciousness and kindness went largely unheeded.

Opposite: Michael performs in Minnesota during the Bad tour.

Opposite and above: Michael, pictured at a PR event staged by Pepsi-Cola, sponsors of the Bad tour. It was the eve of the 1988 Grammy Awards, for which Michael had high hopes, having been nominated in four categories: Album of the Year, Best Male Pop Vocal Performance, Best Male R&B Vocal Performance, and Producer of the Year. He lost out in each case, to U2's *The Joshua Tree*, Sting, Smokey Robinson, and Narada Michael Walden respectively. Michael did wow the audience with two numbers, a slow version of "The Way You Make Me Feel," followed by a terrific rendition of "Man In The Mirror," complete with gospel choir.

Opposite: More plaudits for Michael, this time at a CBS awards ceremony, held in Los Angeles in February 1990. *Bad* may have fallen short of his high expectations, but Jackson remained the jewel in CBS's crown—or, rather, Sony's, for that company had bought out CBS in 1988. Michael's brothers were not faring quite so well. There were plans for a multi-million dollar tour, but the Jacksons could only attract that kind of money with Michael on board. When the project failed to materialize, the brothers repaired to the studio and put together a new album, *2300 Jackson Street*, named after their Gary home. It didn't sell well, even though Michael featured on the title track. The Jacksons' CBS contract was not renewed, and the brothers went their separate ways.

Above: Michael returned to the White House in April 1990, six years after Ronald Reagan honored the star for allowing "Beat It" to be used as part of an anti-drink-driving campaign. On this occasion President George Bush bestowed upon Michael the title Artist of the Decade, referring to his good works as well as his enormous contribution to popular music. There would be yet another presidential award in 1992, with Michael given the honorary title Point of Light Ambassador for his efforts in helping disadvantaged children.

Opposite and above: Michael is guest of honor at the 1990 opening of Donald Trump's Taj Mahal hotel-casino in Atlantic City. He had neither the inclination nor the need to gamble; Michael's fortune was made on the back of his unique talent. He already had one of the best deals in show business with CBS, and when the contract was renewed under the new Sony banner in 1991, Michael stoked up his bank balance still further. A 25 percent royalty rate and various other package sweeteners didn't quite add up the billion-dollar windfall claimed in the press—a string of *Thrillers* would have been required to achieve that—but it was worth around $50 million to the star.

Opposite: The gossip columnists and paparazzi went into meltdown when Michael accompanied Madonna to the 1991 Academy Awards ceremony. Michael led the applause as a Marilynesque Madonna stole the show with a vampish performance of Stephen Sondheim's Oscar-winning song "Sooner Or Later (I Always Get My Man)," which featured in the movie *Dick Tracy*. But this was pragmatism, not romance: it made perfect sense for the two biggest pop stars on the planet to join forces and make one enormous splash. The duet between the two that had been mooted for Michael's next album failed to materialize.

Above: Michael, pictured during a Pepsi-Cola press conference, February 1992. It was announced that Pepsi would once again sponsor the star when he took to the road, stumping up some $20 million to cover the forthcoming Dangerous tour.

Above: Michael was treated like royalty when he embarked on a goodwill tour of Africa in February 1992, part of the Black History Month celebrations. The highlight came during a visit to the Ivory Coast, where he was crowned King of Sani in a special ceremony organized by local tribesmen. Jackson is pictured with a group of orphaned and abandoned children, whom he invited to his hotel in Abidjan.

Opposite: Michael denied allegations that he had undergone treatment to lighten his skin. He claimed any change in skin tone was due to vitiligo, a hereditary disorder that had a bleaching effect on the pigment. In fact, he had been using skin-lightening creams for some considerable time, though he continued to assert his cultural roots: "I am a black American."

Opposite and below: On stage during the Dangerous tour, which began in Munich, Germany, on June 27, 1992 and ran through to November the following year. The album of the same name had had a four-week run at the top of the American chart in December 1991 and was the top-selling long-player of 1992. Michael said he had a particular vision for the follow-up to *Bad*. "I wanted to do an album that was like Tchaikovsky's 'Nutcracker Suite,' so that in a thousand years from now, people would still be listening to it. Something that would live forever. I would like to see children and teenagers and parents and all races all over the world, hundreds and hundreds of years from now, still pulling out songs from that album and dissecting it. I want it to live." *Dangerous* certainly had a significant lifespan in terms of singles success, yielding eight singles that reached the top 30 in the *Billboard* chart, outstripping *Thriller* on that score.

Opposite and above: On stage at Wembley, London, during the Dangerous tour. A highlight of the Dangerous tour—at least for one lucky lady—was Michael's rendition of "She's Out Of My Life." A girl would be plucked from the audience to share the stage with him during the performance of a moving ballad that had been a set-list favorite for over a decade. Dancing close with Michael Jackson while being serenaded was often too much for the chosen few. They wanted to hold the superstar as tightly as possible, and he had to be deft with the microphone in order to deliver the vocals. No doubt the girls pinched themselves when they retook their seats, and no doubt their friends couldn't wait to touch the hand of someone who had touched Michael Jackson.

Opposite: As ever with Michael Jackson shows, the visual effects were as impressive as the music. For the Dangerous tour Michael made a spectacular entry, catapulted onto the empty stage in a move dubbed the "toaster." The crowds went wild as he popped up out of the swirling smoke, seemingly from nowhere. The exit topped that, Michael zooming out of the auditorium by jet pack. Or, at least, that was how it appeared. In fact, it was an illusion devised by the celebrated magician David Copperfield, but the fans lapped up an unforgettable piece of theater.

Above: Washington, January 20, 1993. Bill Clinton greets Michael on stage at his inaugural concert, having just been sworn in as 42nd president of the United States of America. Fleetwood Mac re-formed for the occasion, a coup matched only by having Michael Jackson on the bill. Michael performed "Heal The World" and "Gone Too Soon," another track from the *Dangerous* album. The latter song was dedicated to teenager Ryan White, an AIDS sufferer whom the singer befriended during his battle to be allowed to attend school. In championing Ryan's cause, Michael played a part in changing the law. Legislation improving the care available to AIDS sufferers was passed in 1990, the year Ryan died.

(left to right) Chelsea Clinton, President Bill Clinton, Michael, Fleetwood Mac's Stevie Nicks.

Above and opposite: Michael at the 1993 Grammy Awards with Brooke Shields (opposite). He received a Legend award from sister Janet (above), who said she was delighted "to honor the man I love and admire as an artist and a person." In his acceptance speech Michael dealt with the perception of him portrayed in some parts of the media. "I don't read all the things written about me. I wasn't aware that the world thought I was so weird and bizarre, but when you grow up as I did in front of 100 million people since the age of five, you're automatically different." He added: "My childhood was taken away from me … exchanged for hard work, struggle, and pain."

Below and opposite: Performing at the 27th Superbowl, January 31, 1993. Michael carried the entire halftime show in one of the most prestigious slots in show business, rocking the Pasadena Rose Bowl to the rafters with "Jam," "Billie Jean," and "Black or White." Rival network Fox knew they were onto a loser and made no attempt to beef up their schedule.

Opposite and above: Blowing away the 100,000-strong crowd at the 1993 Superbowl, and basking in the adulation thereafter. The mood was very different a few days later, when Michael subjected himself to primetime probing on the *Oprah Winfrey Show*. Interviewed at Neverland, he spoke about suffering from the skin disease vitiligo, debunked the oxygen chamber story, admitted to just two bouts of plastic surgery, and described Brooke Shields as his current girlfriend. He was coy when asked if he was still a virgin, though. "I'm a gentleman," was all that Oprah could prise out of him.

Opposite and above: The King of Pop weds the King's daughter. Michael, pictured on stage in New York and in Paris with his new wife Lisa Marie Presley, whom he married on May 26, 1994. They had met briefly when Lisa Marie's father, the legendary Elvis Presley, took her to see a Jackson 5 show in the early 70s. The two met again at a dinner party early in 1993 and started dating, the affair intensifying when the storm of the abuse allegations involving Jordan Chandler broke that August. Some thought the marriage was a cynical ploy to restore Jackson's reputation, but he and Lisa Marie did share a grand passion, albeit one destined not to last.

Right: The inimitable Slash joins Michael on stage at the MTV Video Music Awards, held in Los Angeles, September 7, 1995. The Guns 'n' Roses axeman had performed with Michael in a couple of shows during the Dangerous tour, doing some trademark shredding on "Black or White." The two reprised that party piece, while Michael also had the audience in raptures with a medley of classic hits.

Opposite and above: Michael performs a slick quick-change routine at the 1995 MTV Video Awards, casting off in a flash the spangly jacket and loose-fitting shirt worn for the "Billie Jean" segment and turning himself into the besuited troupe leader for a mesmerizing "Dangerous" routine. He ended the evening with yet another clutch of awards. His *Scream* video, a collaboration with sister Janet, was nominated in 11 categories and walked off with the top prize in three of them: Best Dance Video, Best Choreography, and Best Art Direction. A Grammy would follow five months later.

Above: On stage during the MTV Video Awards, September 7, 1995.

Opposite: In December 1995 Michael was due to star in a cable TV special, with illustrious mime artist Marcel Marceau appearing as a guest performer. At rehearsals 72-year-old Marceau, decked out in his trademark Bip the Clown costume, did a spot of moonwalking, while Michael performed the other's famous "invisible wall" routine. The show was canceled when Michael collapsed on stage and had to be hospitalized. He thus never got to perform with one of his heroes, the man who had a profound influence on his own dance style. On hearing the news of Marceau's death in 2007, Michael recalled watching him perform in the 1970s. "I used to sneak in and sit in the audience and watch how he would defy the laws of gravity, like he was stepping on air. I would take some of those things and include it into rhythm and dance when I moved."

Opposite: Basketball legend Earvin "Magic" Johnson got to know the Jackson family through Jackie and Marlon, who were fans of the LA Lakers, the team for which he starred. Michael gave Johnson a cameo role in the Egyptian-themed video of "Remember The Time," the second single release from *Dangerous* in 1991. Johnson had just revealed that he had tested HIV-positive, which raised concerns with some of his fellow NBA professionals, but not with Michael, who had nothing but compassion for those in such a plight. Johnson paid a warm tribute at Michael's memorial service, raising a smile when he recounted how they discussed plans for the video over a bucket of Kentucky Fried Chicken.

Above: Shooting the video for "They Don't Care About Us" in a Rio de Janeiro shantytown. Directed by Spike Lee, the video sparked something of a furor as government officials were concerned that it showed the city in a poor light.

CHAPTER FOUR

HIStory Maker

Above: Three months after "irreconcilable differences" brought his marriage to Lisa Marie Presley to an end in August 1996, Michael tied the knot with 37-year-old divorcée Debbie Rowe. They had known each other for over a decade, having met at the offices of Michael's dermatologist, where Debbie worked as a nursing assistant. Michael's keenness to become a father had been a bone of contention with Lisa Marie, who had two children from her first marriage. Debbie would have no such reservations.

Opposite: Auckland, New Zealand, November, 10 1996. The HIStory tour had been packing theaters since it kicked off in Prague two months earlier. The double album was on its way to becoming the biggest-selling multiple-disk ever, and the world waited to see what visual treats Jackson had in store when he took the show on the road. It was every bit as dazzling as its predecessors, and some thought the sets, costumes, choreography, special effects, and light show raised a bar that had already been set at a dauntingly high level. In fact, the razzmatazz started even before the first sound check: 30-foott-high statues of the singer were floated up some of Europe's main waterways to promote both the album and the tour.

Above and opposite: On stage in Auckand during the HIStory tour (above) and at Wembley, London (opposite). The first single release from the HIStory album was "Scream," which entered the *Billboard* Hot 100 at number 5. That was a chart record but not for long, for the follow up "You Are Not Alone" debuted at number one, an unrivaled achievement. Much of the new material on the album was inspired by Jackson's recent treatment, at the hands of the legal system and the media. In "Tabloid Junkie" he spat out vitriol born of contempt and frustration: "You're a parasite in black and white, do anything for news." "D.S.", meanwhile, was a rancorous attack on the district attorney who led the 1993 child abuse investigation, which folded owing to lack of evidence. Michael would refer to the song "Childhood" as the most honest, most autobiographical he'd ever written.

Above: Michael joined an elite group of pop music greats when he was inducted into the Rock and Roll Hall of Fame for the second time in 2001. On that occasion he was being honored as a solo artist. Four years earlier he entered the Hall of Fame as a member of The Jackson 5. He is pictured receiving that award, along with fellow inductees the Bee Gees. Diana Ross looks on proudly at the singer she took under her wing when he was a youth.

Opposite: No sooner had the furore over the child abuse allegations died down than Michael found himself front-page news in the tabloid press once again. In November 1996, with the HIStory tour in full swing, it was revealed that Debbie Rowe was carrying Michael's baby. The advancement of the pregnancy confirmed that she had conceived before Michael's divorce from Lisa Marie was finalized. Prince Michael Jackson Jr. was born February 13, 1997; daughter Paris Michael Katherine Jackson arrived on April 3 the following year.

Opposite: Tokyo, July 1999. Michael announces the formation of Michael Jackson Japan Company Ltd, a billion-dollar worldwide entertainment business that would have charitable giving as a central plank of its corporate strategy.

Above: Sun City, September 4, 1999. Former South African president Nelson Mandela leads the applause as Michael is presented with a lifetime achievement award. If professional honors continued to be heaped upon him, Michael's private life was still in tumult. A month later divorce papers were filed, ending his marriage to Debbie Rowe. The cares of the world obviously weighed heavily upon him, but he found strength from a predictable source: "If it wasn't for the children I'd throw in the towel." Michael was awarded custody of Prince Michael Jr. and Paris.

Opposite: New York, March 19, 2001. Michael is inducted into the Rock and Roll Hall of Fame for the second time, at 42 one of the youngest solo artists to be thus honored.

Above: Michael makes a surprise guest appearance at the 2001 MTV Awards, joining multiple winners 'N Sync on stage. One of hottest boy bands around and with Justin Timberlake in their number, 'N Sync scooped four awards that night, but Jackson gave a scene-stealing cameo, bursting out of an Etch-A-Sketch backdrop to light up the group's performance with some of his trademark moves.

Above: New York, September 7, 2001. The Jacksons arriving at Madison Square Garden for the concert marking Michael's 30 years as a solo artist.

Opposite: Long-time friend and confidant Elizabeth Taylor pictured with Michael at the 30th anniversary gala concert. It was Taylor who dubbed Michael "The King of Pop, Rock, and Soul" when she introduced him at a 1989 awards ceremony, a moniker that stuck in its truncated form.

Opposite, above and following pages: Celebrating Michael's 30th anniversary as a solo artist. The Jackson brothers rolled back the years with a medley of hits including "ABC" and "I'll Be There." "Michael introduced "I Want You Back," saying they would perform it as they had done on the *Ed Sullivan Show* in 1969. Guests included 'N Sync, who strutted their stuff for Dancing Machine, and Usher, who joined Michael during the rendition of his latest single "You Rock My World," from the album *Invincible*. The latter would be his

Above: Michael is dubbed "Artist of the Millennium" at the 2002 MTV Awards. It wasn't a formal honor, just part of Britney Spears's eulogy as she brought Michael on stage to receive a cake to mark his 44th birthday. He gave an acceptance speech based on the lofty title and confusion reigned. It hardly mattered; most of the audience would probably have agreed with the ranking Britney bestowed upon him.

Opposite: Michael and Elizabeth Taylor arrive at the wedding of Liza Minnelli and David Gest at the Marble Collegiate Church in New York on March 16, 2002. Michael was to give Minnelli away and serve as co-best man and Elizabeth Taylor was a co-maid of honor.

Above: Michael poses with the Reverend Jesse Jackson at the National Broadcasting Convention in Chicago, June 2003. Michael's faith was a bulwark of his life, something he would need to sustain him in what would prove to be a testing year. A television documentary, *Living With Michael Jackson*, did him no favors, especially the admission that he had indeed shared a bed with children on numerous occasions. He would read them stories and fetch hot milk; it was "sweet" and "charming." Needless to say, the tabloid press didn't see it that way. Michael went on the offensive, stating that the documentary was "a gross distortion of the truth."

Opposite: Back to where it all started. In June 2003 Gary's most famous son returned to his hometown for the first time in 20 years.

Below: With his older sister La Toya at the 2003 Black Entertainment Television Awards, held at the Kodak Center, Los Angeles on June 24. The entire schedule for the 2009 BET Awards was changed at the last minute when news of Michael's death reached the producers. It became instead a tribute to the King of Pop.

Opposite: Michael's chief duty at the BET ceremony was to present James Brown with a Lifetime Achievement award. 50 Cent might have been the big winner on the night, but his success was overshadowed as the King of Pop shared a stage with the Godfather of Soul. As a child Michael would watch Brown's electrifying stage routines on TV and then attempt to copy them. He would rail angrily at the set if there was a close-up and he couldn't see what Brown's twinkling feet were doing. At the awards show Michael did a fizzing little dance routine as a tribute to the man he said had influenced him more than any other. He gave a respectful bow and draped a regal cloak over his hero, but Brown in turn insisted that Michael himself should accept the mantle, for he had developed his own unique style.

Above: Michael celebrates his 45th birthday with fans. Michael's fans remained fiercely loyal in the face of the adverse comment that was regularly served up in the media. His 2001 album *Invincible* sold in millions and went straight to number one on both sides of the Atlantic. It may not have had the longevity of a *Thriller* or *Bad*, but it represented a great success by the standards of the industry's mortals. The fact that *Invincible* was produced at a time when Michael's relationship with Sony was beginning to sour made it an all the more impressive achievement.

Opposite: Michael poses for photographs with the mother of business associate Marc Scaffle at the Aladdin Hotel, Las Vegas, prior to the 2003 Radio Music Awards on October 27, 2003.

Above and opposite: Beyonce presents Michael with a special Humanitarian Award at the 2003 Radio Music Awards ceremony, which was held at the Aladdin Casino Resort, Las Vegas, on October 27. He had won so many awards, Beyonce quipped, that the RMA had to invent a new one just for him. It was given "for your selfless contribution towards making

Left: Radio Music Awards ceremony 2003. With yet another accolade and a new compilation album *Number Ones* just out, it seemed that Michael's life was in good shape. That all changed a few weeks later, when the Santa Barbara Police Department issued a warrant for his arrest on child molestation charges. "His life has been about peace," brother Jermaine said by way of rebuttal, while Michael himself maintained he would "slit his wrists" before he'd hurt a child.

Opposite: In pensive mood just before the storm was about to break. The 1993 scandal surrounding Jordan Chandler ended when the police dropped the case and Michael paid a sum believed to be over $20 million to the "victim's"family. This time the police would press charges and bring the case to court. On November 20, 2003, the day after a warrant for his arrest was issued, Jackson flew to Santa Barbara to be taken into custody. He had his fingerprints and mugshot taken before being released on $3 million bail.

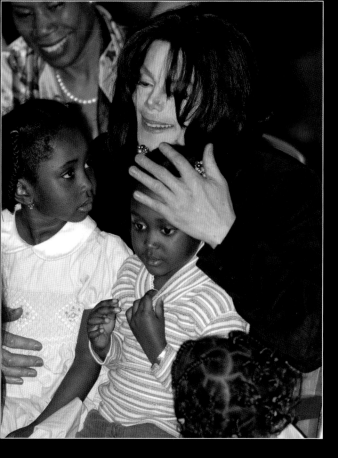

Opposite: Receiving yet another humanitarian award, this time from the African Ambassadors' Spouses Association. The presentation was made at the Ethiopian Embassy, Washington DC, on April 1, 2004. Predictably, the media were more interested in the ongoing legal proceedings—"Good news doesn't sell," as Michael pointed out. In January 2004 he pleaded Not Guilty on seven charges of child molestation. The cloud would hang over his head for a whole year, the time it took for the case to come to trial.

Above: Michael embraces the children who performed for him during the award ceremony at the Embassy.

Opposite and above: Michael, surrounded by family and friends at his arraignment, January 16, 2004. Seven months later, August 16, he gives a defiant gesture as he arrives at Santa Maria courthouse for the pre-trial hearing (opposite). "If I am guilty of anything, it is giving all that I have to help children all over the world."

Above and opposite: Washington DC, March 2004. Michael meets Republican Congresswoman Sheila Jackson-Lee and a group of African ambassadors to discuss HIV-Aids. Recalling that meeting in the speech she delivered at Michael's memorial service, Jackson-Lee said that watching him hold forth on an issue he cared so deeply about was "a miraculous experience. He was the Good Samaritan," she said; "Michael never stopped giving."

Opposite: Michael arrives at the Santa Maria courthouse with his entourage.

Right: The strain is etched on Michael's face as the trial proceeds in spring 2005. Drawn and thin, his haunted appearance is matched by a weak voice that was cracked and uncertain. On two occasions he needed medical attention, and Judge Rodney Melville even threatened to revoke his bail and have him confined after he shuffled into the courtroom an hour late wearing pajamas. Outside, fans brandished placards pledging their support and loyalty.

Opposite: Michael, pictured with his lead counsel Thomas Mesereau Jr as the trial draws to a close. Elizabeth Taylor and Diana Ross were among the star-studded list of possible defense witnesses, though in the event neither was called, and Jackson himself did not testify. Macaulay Culkin, who featured in the *Black Or White* video when he was 11 years old, did give evidence. He said he had shared Jackson's bed—quite innocently. "He's just a guy who is actually very kid-like himself," said the star of the *Home Alone* movies.

Above: Santa Maria, California, June 3: Sisters Janet (center) and La Toya (left) arrive to hear the closing arguments in the six-month trial.

Above: Joseph Jackson accompanies his son into the courthouse. All the family offered their support, though Michael's mother Katherine was the mainstay, the only member who attended on each of the 60 days that the trial lasted. She vehemently protested his innocence of all the charges, which included plying a minor with liquor, conspiring to commit child abduction, false imprisonment, and extortion.

Opposite: Michael waves to his supporters.

Opposite and above: June 13, 2005. Katherine Jackson shares her son's relief as he is acquitted on all charges. A Guilty verdict could have meant over 18 years in jail, so there was much to celebrate. But it was left to the fans that had gathered outside to start the party; the stress of the trial had taken a severe toll on Michael, who looked a pale shadow of the person who lit up the stage with his vibrant performances.

Below and opposite: There was pandemonium on the streets of London in October 2005 as fans jostled to catch a glimpse of their idol. Many voiced their support, others just screamed. Michael took his three children to see a performance of *Billy Elliot* at the Victoria Palace Theatre, and the itinerary also included a visit to Madame Tussauds and a shopping expedition to Harrods. Security was tight, but a few lucky fans got a prized autograph.

Opposite: Tokyo, May 27, 2006. Michael's appearance at the MTV Awards sends the 8,000-strong Yoyogi National Stadium audience into raptures. He paid tribute to his fans in Japan and across the world as he accepted his Legend Award. Such ceremonies showed the esteem and affection the public still had for Michael, though they contributed little to his coffers. A month prior to the Japan trip he had been forced to relinquish control of the coveted Beatles catalogue. He had already sold a 50 percent stake to Sony back in the mid-1990s, and subsequently used his half-share as collateral to raise $200 million.

Above: Arriving at the World Music Awards, held at Earls Court, London, on November 15, 2006.

Left and opposite: At the 2006 World Music Awards Michael picked up the Diamond Award, given to artists with album sales in excess of 100 million. Michael had hit that mark with *Thriller* alone, and in honor of that achievement Chris Brown led a troupe that recreated the famous title track video routine. Michael joined a children's choir for a rendition of "We Are The World," which had helped raise over $60 million for famine relief. He left minus his sparkly jacket, though, having tossed it into a febrile crowd to be fought over by trophy-hunters.

Above: Michael receives the Diamond Award—and a warm embrace—from Beyonce. "If it wasn't for Michael Jackson," she said in her introductory remarks, "I would never have performed. He's made such an impact on my life, and every performer's life." Beyonce quoted two staggering statistics: album sales in excess of 750 million, and over $300 million donated to charity. "Return of the King" ran the legend on one placard.

Opposite: Michael pictured giving thanks for the award.

Above and opposite: Marking the passing of the Godfather of Soul. Michael is consoled by Reverend Al Sharpton, and (opposite) gives a personal tribute to his hero James Brown, who died on Christmas Day 2006. Michael said that as a child he would stop whatever he was doing to watch Brown perform on television. Seeing the "master at work" convinced Michael that show business was the only avenue he wanted to pursue.

Opposite and above: O2 Arena, London,
March 5, 2009. The auditorium is packed for the
briefest of appearances by Michael as he announces
his long-awaited return to live performance. There
were to be 10 shows, later extended to 50 dates. "This
is it," was Michael's refrain, "the final curtain call"; it
would be the last time he would perform in London.
Comeback tours abound in popular music, and "last
chance to see" claims are rarely set in stone. Whether
it was hype or fact, the concerts sold out in five hours.

Above: Michael attends a performance of *Oliver!* at London's Drury Lane Theatre on the day following the announcement of the O2 concerts. The extended tour was not merely to satisfy the obvious demand. Michael's extravagant lifestyle, his retinue, and his unstinting generosity had left a hole in his finances. Neverland, the fantasy playground where he had entertained so many sick children, cost over $1 million per month to run. That was now gone. Michael moved into a rental property in Bel Air, at a cost of some $100,000 per month.

Opposite: This publicity photograph, showing Michael rehearsing for the forthcoming shows at the Staples Center in Los Angeles, was circulated in June 2009 by tour sponsors AEG. The impression it created, of a fit, confident performer back on top of his game, may not have been completely accurate. When the first four shows were postponed, the official line was the need for more rehearsal time, but questions over Michael's state of health were also raised.

Right: Checking out some camera shots with Kenny Ortega, director of the This Is It tour and a man who had helped create a number of Michael's shows over the years. At Michael's memorial service he waxed lyrical about the concert no one would now see. Michael suffered a suspected heart attack just after noon on June 25, 2009. He was rushed to the Ronald Reagan UCLA Medical Center, where he was pronounced dead at 2:26pm. Kenny Ortega said that the new show would have been "his greatest personal work," an event that would have signaled "his triumphant return to the world." Michael Jackson was "timeless and timely, musical and magical."

Below: Berry Gordy offers condolences to Katherine Jackson at Michael's memorial concert on July 7, 2009. Gordy, the Motown boss who launched Michael's career when he signed The Jackson 5 in 1968, voiced the opinion of many when he spoke of Michael's contribution to popular music. "He studied the greats and became greater. He raised the bar, and then broke the bar. His talent and creativity thrust him and entertainment into another stratosphere."

Above: Jermaine Jackson performs one of Michael's favorite songs, "Smile," at his brother's memorial concert, held at the Staples Center. Michael had included the Charlie Chaplin-penned song on the *HIStory* album and planned to release it as a single at one stage. Other tributes included a message from Nelson Mandela, read by Smokey Robinson. "Michael was a giant and a legend in the music industry, and we mourn with the millions of fans worldwide. We also mourn with his family and his friends over the loss of our dear friend." Congresswoman Sheila Jackson-Lee, who had been so moved by Michael's efforts in the battle against HIV-Aids, said that a resolution would be introduced into the House of Representatives, citing Michael Jackson as "an American legend and musical icon, a world humanitarian, someone who will be honored forever."

Above: A family united in grief. Michael's daughter Paris and elder son Prince Michael I join (left to right) Janet, La Toya and Jermaine on stage for a moving finale to the memorial service. Paris held back the tears just long enough to pay her own personal tribute. "Ever since I was born, Daddy has been the best father you could ever imagine, and I just wanted to say I love him so much."

Above: Members of the Jackson family and close friends, including singers Lionel Richie (third from the left) and Jennifer Hudson (second from the right), perform "We Are The World," a song born out of empathy for those in desperate circumstances that perhaps best reflects Michael's enormous talent and his generosity of spirit.

Left: Michael's brothers act as pall bearers to the sibling who outshone them all. Even the regal title King of Pop didn't do him justice, said Berry Gordy. "I think he is simply the greatest entertainer that ever lived."

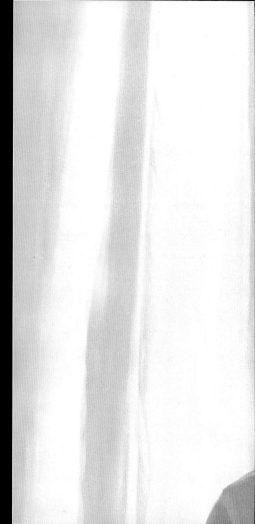

Chronology
& Discography

1958 – Michael Joseph Jackson is born August 29 in Gary, Indiana, to Joseph and Katherine Jackson, the seventh of nine children.

1962 – Michael, aged four, joins older brothers Jackie, Tito, and Jermaine, who perform as The Jackson Brothers. Five-year-old Marlon also joins the line-up. The group begins to gain success on the talent competition circuit.

1967 – Now performing as The Jackson 5, the group wins a prestigious amateur contest at the Apollo Theater, Harlem, impressing Motown star Gladys Knight.

1968 – The group record their first single, "Big Boy," for the Gary-based Steeltown label. It becomes a hit on the local airwaves. The Jackson 5 sign to Motown after Berry Gordy views a tape of the audition.

1969 – After a year of recording and being groomed by Motown, the group's debut single "I Want You Back" is released in October. Their first album, *Diana Ross Presents The Jackson 5*, is issued two months later.

1970 – "I Want You Back" goes to number one on the *Billboard* Hot 100. Follow-up singles "ABC," "The Love You Save," and "I'll Be There" also top the charts, the first time in history that a group's first four releases had gone to number one.

1971– Michael launches his solo career with "Got to Be There," a top five hit in the US.

1972 – Michael scores his first number one single as a solo artist with "Ben."

1976 – After 8 years, a string of hit singles and 14 albums, the Jacksons leave Motown and sign to Epic. Jermaine, who is married to Berry Gordy's daughter, remains with the Detroit label. For legal reasons, the group are rebranded as The Jacksons.

1978 – The Jacksons have a hit with the *Destiny* album, following a lukewarm reception for their first two long-players on the Epic label. Michael makes his film debut, playing the Scarecrow opposite Diana Ross in *The Wiz*, an all-black production of *The Wizard of Oz*. He befriends Quincy Jones, the movie's musical director.

1979 – Releases *Off the Wall*, his first solo collaboration with Quincy Jones. The album yields four top-ten hits in the US and goes platinum.

1981 – Michael joins his brothers for the Triumph Tour, but is increasingly preoccupied with solo projects.

1982 – Releases *Thriller*, the fruit of another collaboration with Quincy Jones, which tops the chart for 37 weeks. Seven of the nine tracks are top 10 hits in the US, and it becomes the biggest-selling album of all time, eventually breaking the 100 million barrier.

1983 – Michael unveils his signature move the moonwalk while performing Billie Jean in a television special to mark Motown's 25th anniversary. A 16-year-old street dancer taught him how to do it.

1984 – *Thriller* receives seven Grammy Awards, and Michael adds an eighth to his haul for his children's recording of *E.T. The Extra-Terrestrial*. The groundbreaking video of the title track becomes an instant MTV hit, widely acknowledged as the best the best music video of all time. Michael suffers second-degree burns to the scalp while making a Pepsi-Cola commercial. Joins his brothers for the *Victory* album and tour.

1985 – "We Are The World," co-written with Lionel Richie becomes a worldwide hit and raises millions of dollars for famine relief in Africa.

1987 – Releases *Bad*, which yields a record five number-one hits in the US.

1988 – Michael buys a 2700-acre ranch in California and turns it into "Neverland," an amusement park filled with rides, animals, and a movie theater.

1991 – Releases *Dangerous*, which yields another crop of hit singles, including the chart-topping "Black or White." Signs a new deal with Sony, worth a record $65 million.

1992 – Establishes the Heal The World foundation, a charitable organization whose aim is to improve the lot of disadvantaged children across the world.

1993 – There is a police investigation after 13-year-old Jordan Chandler accuses Michael of molestation. The case is dropped due to lack of evidence. Reveals in a TV interview with Oprah Winfrey that he suffers from the hereditary disorder vitiligo, which accounts for the change in skin tone .

1994 – Marries Lisa Marie Presley, daughter of Elvis. The marriage ends 19 months later. A sum in excess of $20 million is paid to the Chandler family.

1995 – Releases *HIStory: Past, Present and Future, Book 1*, a two-CD set featuring new material and a selection of greatest hits. "You Are Not Alone" tops the charts but the record is generally perceived as a disappointment.

1996 – Michael marries Debbie Rowe, a nurse who worked at his dermatologist's practice. She is already pregnant with their child.

1997 – Prince Michael Jackson Jr. born February 13. Releases the remix album *Blood On The Dancefloor*.

1998 – Daughter Paris Michael Katherine Jackson born April 3.

1999 – The couple divorce, Michael gaining custody of the children.

2001 – Michael is inducted into the Rock and Roll Hall of Fame as a solo artist, having already joined that exclusive club as a member of The Jackson 5. Performs with his brothers at a Madison Square Garden celebrating the 30th anniversary of his first solo record. Releases *Invincible*, which hits top spot in the album chart but fades quickly.

2002 – A second son, Prince Michael Jackson II, born. Known as Blanket, the identity of the child's mother is not revealed. Jackson is criticized for dangling Prince Michael II from a hotel balcony in Germany. Upset with Sony over the promotion given to *Invincible*, Michael lambasts corporation boss Tommy Mottola, calling him "devilish."

2003 –The Santa Barbara police issue a warrant for Jackson's arrest on child molestation charges. Michael admits to sharing a bed with children in a TV documentary. The compilation album *Number Ones* hits is released.

2004 – Jackson pleads not guilty to all charges, which include false imprisonment, extortion, and supplying a minor with alcohol. He is released on $3 million bail.

2005 – Following a trial lasting four-months, Jackson is acquitted on all charges. A new compilation album *The Essential Michael Jackson* is released. It only just breaks into the top 100 in the United States but is more successful outside the US.

2009 – Michael announces that he will perform 10 shows at London's O2 arena in July, later extended to 50 concerts. Tickets sell out within 5 hours of being released. On June 25, Jackson suffers a suspected cardiac arrest at his Bel Air home. He is rushed to UCLA Medical Center, where he is pronounced dead at 2:26 pm. A memorial service is held at the Staples Center, Los Angeles on July 7 to mourn the passing and celebrate the life of the King of Pop.

ALBUMS

THE JACKSON 5

1969: Diana Ross Presents The Jackson 5

1970: ABC

1970: Third Album

1970: The Jackson 5 Christmas Album

1971: Maybe Tomorrow

1971: Goin' Back to Indiana

1972: Lookin' Through the Windows

1973: Skywriter

1973: The Jackson 5 in Japan

1973: G.I.T.: Get It Together

1974: Dancing Machine

1975: Moving Violation

1976: The Jacksons

1977: Goin' Places

1978: Destiny

1980: Triumph

1981: The Jacksons Live!

1984: Victory

1989: 2300 Jackson Street

1992: The Jacksons: An American Dream Soundtrack

MICHAEL JACKSON

1972: Got to Be There

1972: Ben

1973: Music & Me

1975: Forever, Michael

1979: Off the Wall

1982: Thriller

1987: Bad

1991: Dangerous

1995: HIStory: Past, Present and Future, Book 1

1997: Blood on the Dancefloor: HIStory in the mix

2001: Invincible

SINGLES

THE JACKSON 5

Steeltown releases:

1968: Big Boy/You've Changed

1968: We Don't Have To Be Over 21 (to Fall in Love)/Jam Session

1968: Let Me Carry Your School Books/ I Never Had A Girl

Dynamo releases:

1969: We Don't Have To Be Over 21 (to Fall in Love)/Some Girls Want Me For Their Lover

Motown releases:

1969: I Want You Back

1970: ABC

1970: The Love You Save

1970: I'll Be There

1970: Santa Claus Is Coming to Town

1970: I Saw Mommy Kissing Santa Claus

1971: Mama's Pearl

1971: Never Can Say Goodbye

1971: Maybe Tomorrow

1971: Sugar Daddy

1972: Little Bitty Pretty One

1972: Lookin' Through the Windows

1972: Doctor My Eyes

1972: Corner of the Sky

1973: Hallelujah Day

1973: Skywriter

1973: Get It Together

1974: The Boogie Man

1974: Dancing Machine

1974: Whatever You Got I Want

1974: Life Of The Party

1974: I Am Love (Part 1)

1975: Forever Came Today

1975: All I Do Is Think of You (B-side of Forever Came Today)

CBS Releases (The Jacksons):

1976: Enjoy Yourself

1977: Show You the Way to Go

1977: Dreamer

1977: Goin' Places

1977: Even Though You're Gone

1978: Different Kind of Lady

1978: Music's Taking Over

1978: Find Me a Girl

1978: Blame It on the Boogie

1979: Shake Your Body (Down to the Ground)

1979: Destiny

1980: Lovely One

1980: This Place Hotel

1981: Can You Feel It

1981: Walk Right Now

1981: Time Waits For No One

1981: Things I Do For You

1984: State of Shock

1984: Torture

1984: Body

1984: Wait

1987: Time Out for The Burglar

1988: 2300 Jackson Street

1989: Nothing (That Compares 2 You)

1989: Art Of Madness

MICHAEL JACKSON

1968: Let Me Carry Your School Books

1971: Got To Be There

1972: Rockin' Robin

1972: I Wanna Be Where You Are

1972: Ain't No Sunshine

1972: Ben

1973: With a Child's Heart

1973: Music and Me

1973: Happy

1975: We're Almost There

1975: Just a Little Bit of You

1979: You Can't Win

1979: Don't Stop Till You Get Enough

1979: Rock With You

1980: Off The Wall

1980: She's Out Of My Life

1980: Girlfriend

1981: One Day In Your Life

1982: The Girl Is Mine
(with Paul McCartney)

1983: Billie Jean

1983: Beat It

1983: Wanna Be Startin' Something

1983: Human Nature

1983: P.Y.T. (Pretty Young Thing)

1984: Thriller

1984: Farewell My Summer Love

1984: Girl You're So Together

1987: I Just Can't Stop Loving You

1987: Bad

1988: The Way You Make Me Feel

1988: Man In The Mirror

1988: Dirty Diana

1988: Another Part Of Me

1988: Smooth Criminal

1989: Leave Me Alone

1989: Liberian Girl

1989: Speed Demon

1991: Black Or White

1992: Remember The Time/
Come Together

1992: In The Closet

1992: Who Is It

1992: Jam

1992: Heal The World

1993: Give In To Me

1993: Will You Be There

1993: Gone Too Soon

1993: Dangerous

1995: Scream

1995: You Are Not Alone

1995: Earth Song

1996: This Time Around (with Notorious B.I.G)

1996: They Don't Care About Us

1996: Stranger In Moscow

1997: Smile

1997: Blood On The Dancefloor

1997: HIStory/Ghosts

1997: Is It Scary

2001: You Rock My World

2001: Cry

2002: Butterflies

2002: Heaven Can Wait

2003: What More Can I Give

2003: One More Chance

COMPILATIONS

THE JACKSON 5

Motown releases:

1971: Greatest Hits

1976: Anthology

1976: Joyful Jukebox Music

1976: Boogie

1995: Soulsation!

1995: Jackson 5—The Ultimate Collection

CBS releases:

2004: The Essential Jacksons

2004: The Very Best of The Jacksons

Other releases:

1993: Children of the Light

1999: The Steeltown Sessions

2007: The Jacksons' Story

MICHAEL JACKSON

1975: The Best of Michael Jackson

1981: One Day in Your Life

1983: 18 Greatest Hits

1983: 9 Singles Pack

1984: 14 Greatest Hits

1987: Love Songs (with Diana Ross)

1988: Singles Souvenir Pack

1992: Motown's Greatest Hits

1992: Tour Souvenir Pack

1997: The Best of Michael Jackson & The Jackson 5ive

1999: The Very Best of Michael Jackson with The Jackson Five

2000: 20th Century Masters—The Millennium Collection: The Best of Michael Jackson

2001: Greatest Hits: HIStory, Vol. 1

2003: Number Ones

2004: Off the Wall/Thriller

2004: Bad/Dangerous

2004: Michael Jackson: The Ultimate Collection

2005: The Essential Michael Jackson

2008: King of Pop

2008: Gold

2008: 50 Best Songs: The Motown Years

2008: Dangerous/Dangerous—The Short Films

2009: The Collection

2009: The Hits

Thank you to Hayley Newman and Martina Oliver at Getty Images, and also to Alice Hill and Wendy Toole for their help in producing this book.